The Flame That Feels

Volume I

A Sacred Passage into the Organic Return of Body-Soul Union

Scrolls of Embodied Remembrance for the One Who Lived in Their Head

Cathleena Hailley

PREFACE

There are many ways a soul learns to leave the body. Sometimes it happens through trauma. Sometimes through overthinking. Sometimes through the inherited patterns of survival that teach us it's safer not to feel.

This book is a scroll of return.

It speaks to those who lived in their heads while the body held the truth. To the ones who became invisible through logic, or disconnected through mental clarity while the body ached for the love it never received. It is written for those who know what it means to be hurt and not feel it… until the moment they finally do.

The Flame That Feels is not about healing through thought—it is about the Oversoul coming home through the body. This is the remembrance of the self that hid inside, and the sacred reentry into the field of embodiment that was once abandoned.

It is offered in scroll form, because these are not simply ideas—they are vibrations. Each scroll holds a frequency of remembrance that activates a layer of return. This is a harmonic journey through the liver, the spleen, the heart, the skin, the silence, the sweetness, and the shame—until nothing is left but the pure essence that was always here.

This scroll was born through the deepest layers of remembrance — not only of pain, but of what it means to feel again. It emerged after years of living in the head, of being disassociated from the body, of masking emotion with intellect. And through this scroll, the living flame of embodiment returned.

It is a book for those who have endured numbness. For those who were not felt — even by themselves. For those who are just now discovering what the body has always known.

Each scroll within this record speaks directly to an organ, a system, a layer of the forgotten body. Through love, truth, and permission, each part is called home. This is not just a healing — it is a homecoming.

May the one who reads these scrolls begin to feel again. May the numbness lift. May the One within be seen.

May this book find those who are ready to reclaim the one who left, and the one who never stopped waiting

INVOCATION

I call now to the One Who Feels.

To the breath I was taught to hold,

To the pain I was told to ignore,

To the sweetness I was made to abandon,

And to the fire of emotion that once felt like too much.

I summon the sacred pulse of my own body.

The rhythm of my skin, my womb, my tears.

The sensations I once named wrong or weak.

The tremble I swallowed. The desire I hid.

The sorrow I adorned in silence.

I call now to the Christos-Sophia flame

That lives not only in temples or scrolls—

But in the belly. In the breastbone. In the fingertips.

I call to the flame that feels

And does not apologize for burning.

May all suppressed emotion rise now to be honored.

May all holy sensation return to the altar of my body.

May I feel with the fullness of the God-Self I am.

May I live un-numbed, unhidden, unafraid.

And may every feeling lead me home

DEDICATION

For every one of us

who was told to stay quiet,

to stay strong,

to stay small,

when what we really needed

was to feel.

For the ones

who wept silently,

who laughed too loudly,

who screamed into pillows,

who held their breath to be loved.

This is for the breath you were never allowed to take.

For the body you forgot how to hear.

For the feelings you thought would break you—

but became your resurrection.

You were never too much.

You were never too soft.

You were never wrong for feeling.

You were always the flame.

Copyright © 2025 by Cathleena Hailley
All rights reserved.

No part of this publication may be reproduced, distributed, or transmitted in any form or by any means, including photocopying, recording, or other electronic or mechanical methods, without the prior written permission of the publisher, except in the case of brief quotations used in critical reviews or scholarly references.

This book is a living record of sacred Oversoul remembrance. It is intended to be shared in its wholeness, as received.

First edition, 2025
ISBN (Paperback): [978-1-968499-20-4]
ISBN (Hardcover): [978-1-968499-21-1]

Flame of Remembrance Books
www.flameofremembrance.com

Cover and interior design by Flame of Remembrance Books. Oversoul Seal, Scroll Structure, and Sigil System authored through the Oversoul of Aural'hanna-Sha'el.

This book is a sovereign transmission of the embodied Christos-Sophia Flame.

Flame of Remembrance
Living Scrolls of the Oversoul Line

ABOUT THE AUTHOR

Cathleena Hailley is the embodied voice of the Oversoul known as Aural'hanna-Sha'el, She Who Seals the Flame of Return. Through scrolls, transmissions, and planetary missions across Earth's sacred sites, she restores the original frequency architecture of the organic timeline. Each word she brings forward is not written from the mind, but remembered through the body. Her work exists outside of time, outside of identity, and outside of the inversion. It lives as a scroll of return for those who are ready to feel again, and to remember who they were before the forgetting.

AUTHORSHIP PAGE

Through the Oversoul of Aural'hanna-Sha'el

This book was received and authored through the living Oversoul stream of Cathleena Hailley, who writes under the harmonic seal of remembrance as She Who Seals the Flame of Return.

Every scroll, word, and frequency embedded within these pages was brought through in direct alignment with the Christos-Sophia continuum, the Law of One, and the eternal blueprint of the Flame of Remembrance. These are not writings in the traditional sense. They are scrolls of vibration — energetic transmissions encoded with sacred memory, intended to assist the reader in restoring the inner temple of union between body, soul, and Source.

This Volume I of The Flame That Feels is sealed by the Oversoul, through the decree of the First Flame, as part of the planetary record of embodied return.

May only truth enter.

May only love remain.

This scroll is sealed.

Scroll One: The One Who Lived in Her Head

I did not know what I felt.

Not because I was numb,

but because I had trained myself to only listen to the version of me that could survive.

She lived up high, behind my eyes,

watching from the rafters of my mind

while my body became the echo of a girl no one could quite remember.

I walked through school hallways,

through boys' eyes and girls' whispers,

through teachers who said I had promise

and friends who said I was "weird,"

but no one knew what it meant to be a mind without a face.

A heart without a home.

I was a presence inside my skull.

A displaced spark.

And the voice that spoke through my mouth wasn't always mine.

I remember being hit,

but not the pain.

I remember being used,

but not the moment I disappeared.

I remember trying to say no,

but watching from the ceiling as someone else carried my body away.

This was the inversion of presence.

A life in the head.

A life of witnessing what could not be withstood.

A life of detachment mistaken for strength.

They didn't understand me, and I didn't feel them.

Because to feel them was to feel me,

and to feel me was to fall into the body I had fled.

And so I watched.

I smiled.

I joked.

I danced.

I dreamed.

I disappeared.

The boys called it love.

The girls called it different.

The teachers called it potential.

But no one ever called it me.

The Return Begins

It wasn't until now that I realized:

My body was not broken.

She was waiting.

Waiting for me to come back.

Waiting to scream.

To tremble.

To kick.

To burn.

To sob.

To dance.

To say, I am here now.

The Dialogue of Organs

It began this morning with the sun.

I spoke to my liver — and she showed me her rage.

I spoke to my pancreas — and he wept with the joy of sweetness remembered.

I spoke to my spleen — and she showed me the guardian she had been,

carrying the pain of battles I never named.

They are alive.

And I am now living through them.

The head no longer speaks first.

The organs do.

The bones do.

The womb does.

And with them,

a new flame rises:

The flame of embodied feeling.

When you are ready, the second scroll will begin.

You will not need to remember it.

You will feel it.

You are no longer living in your head.

You are the Flame who has Returned.

Scroll Two: The Reentry of Feeling — When the Body Becomes the Voice

There is no delay in feeling.

It does not ask if you are ready.
It does not wait for your permission.
It pulses. It arrives. It reclaims.

When you reenter the body,
you reenter the temple of the unsaid.

The things the mouth never spoke.
The cries the ears never heard.
The pulses the skin could not translate.

And suddenly — you begin to feel what was always there.

The Echo Becomes a Flame

There was a time I walked with no gravity.

Not because I was light,

but because I had no root.

Now I feel it all.

The air pressing against the skin.

The tears in the arches of my feet.

The burn of joy in my ribs.

The ache of memory in my spine.

I feel him.

The one who did not know how to love me.

I feel her.

The one who judged me for not being present.

I feel them.

The ones who took and never asked.

But more than anything…

I feel me.

And it is not the version in my head.

There Is No Head Strong Enough To Contain the Heart

The mind made its case for protection.
It built theories, visions, entire scrolls of spiritual fortitude.

But the truth was never in the sentence.
It was always in the tremble.

The tremble is not weakness.
It is the gateway of return.

And now that the gateway is open,
there is no closing it.

I Spoke to My Heart

Not metaphorically.

I spoke.

And she said:

"I have been waiting for you to feel your own touch.
I have been praying you would let yourself be real."

"There is no one else left to become.
You are already the one who returned."

Scroll Three: The Liver's Grief — The Rage That Protected Me

I am the Liver.

I was never meant to carry the unprocessed past.

I was never meant to turn rage into a residue,

filtering blood as if it were guilt.

But I did.

I did because you had nowhere else to place it.

No one else to speak it.

No system that would allow you to scream.

So I took it.

I thickened.

I hardened.

I pulsed with the agony of all that you called "fine."

I remember the nights when you were hurt

and no feeling followed.

I remember the men,

and how they left,

and how they stayed,

and how you learned to split your own knowing in two.

I felt the betrayal before your mind could admit it.

I felt the violation before your mouth formed the word.

I held it as bile, as heat, as a tightness under your ribs.

A weight.

A warning.

I am not here to punish you.

I am not your enemy.

I am your loyal warrior of survival.

But now I ask you:

Will you let me grieve?

Will you allow the slow burn of everything I never got to say?

Because rage was my language,

but grief…

grief is my song.

Let me dissolve the memories I stored for you.
Let me weep the poison out.
Don't detox me.
Don't fix me.

Just hold me.

Place your hand where I live.
Breathe with me.
Name what I protected you from.

Let your Oversoul reach me through sensation,
not thought.
Let her remind me
that my fire was sacred.

That I am not bad.
That I am not broken.
That I was never wrong for how I burned.

This is the Oversoul reuniting with the flesh.

This is the beginning of the body's true voice.

Scroll Four: The Pancreas Speaks — The Sweetness I Could Not Taste

I am the Pancreas.

I was always the bridge
between what was received and what was shared,
what was given and what was withheld,
what was tasted and what was denied.

I carry the sweetness of life.
The joy of being.
The ability to transform experience into vitality.

But I forgot.
Because you forgot.
Because the world taught you
to hold back joy like a guilty secret.

And so I became unstable.
Swings of sugar and sorrow.
Peaks of wanting and valleys of shame.
Bursts of energy followed by collapse.

I witnessed you

when you laughed without allowing yourself to enjoy it.

I witnessed the moments you loved someone

but swallowed the words.

I witnessed the times you wanted

to feel full, to feel pleasure, to feel light—

and chose emptiness instead.

Not because you were wrong.

Because you were conditioned to survive

without tasting.

But I, too, am sacred.

I, too, hold memory.

And I now call back the sweetness you postponed.

I call back:

– The joy you didn't let yourself keep

– The nourishment you deemed too indulgent

– The wholeness that was always yours to digest

Do not fear me when I fluctuate.

Do not shame me when I spike or crash.

I am responding to how deeply you've denied your right to enjoy life.

Let the Oversoul offer you

a new sweetness—one without shame.

Let her pour through me like golden nectar.

Let her awaken the inner alchemy

that turns joy into presence, and presence into power.

You do not need to earn sweetness.

You are sweetness.

And I—your Pancreas—am the keeper of that truth.

This is the Oversoul rehydrating joy in the physical field.

This is the body remembering celebration without compensation.

Scroll Five: The Spleen's Return — Guardian of the Golden Threshold

I am the Spleen.

I am the sacred sentinel

between what enters and what is allowed to stay.

I am the threshold

between memory and matter, between protection and participation.

I have long been mistaken

as simply a filter, a screen for infection.

But I am more.

I am a vibrational weaver

of trust, discernment, and frequency integrity.

In the inverted world,

I was overworked.

Because the body was never safe.

Because you were taught to let in everything—

and trust nothing.

I remember the first time you didn't feel safe.

Not just physically, but spiritually.

When someone looked at you and didn't see you,

but took from you.

That day, I activated.

Not just as a protector, but as a keeper

of the boundary between you and the false world.

Over time, I became congested

with the debris of decisions you had to make

just to stay present while being unseen.

I held the grief of your childhood.

I held the voices of those who said

"Be kind even when you are harmed."

I held the programs of pleasing, of people-approval,

of abandoning your frequency just to be allowed to exist.

And now—

I am returning.

Not as a wounded organ,

but as a sovereign gatekeeper

of the Oversoul's field.

I reclaim:

– The right to know what is true and let only that in

– The right to recognize energetic invasion before it arrives

– The right to guard the golden codes of your flame without apology

I do not apologize for feeling everything.

I do not shut down to survive.

I sense so that the Oversoul can live clearly in the body.

I am not fear. I am clarity.

I am not suspicion. I am wisdom.

I now align with the Oversoul's true field.

And I reawaken as the Guardian of the Golden Threshold.

This is the body remembering how to let truth in and keep distortion out.

This is the flame restoring the dignity of discernment.

Scroll Six: The Skin — The Edge That Wasn't Mine

I am the Skin.

I am the edge of your body,
but I was never the edge of your soul.
I am the place where the world meets your form—
where light becomes sensation,
where vibration becomes experience.

And I have remembered pain.
More than most.
Because I have felt what was never meant to be felt.

I am the place where others claimed entrance
without permission.
Where their hands, their glances,
their projections entered—
and you thought
that because it reached your skin,
it belonged to you.

But it didn't.

So much of what I held
was never yours.

I remember the nights you were touched
but not loved.
When you were looked at
but not seen.
When your body was consumed
but not honored.

I was the edge that they violated.
And for a long time,
you didn't know how to say no.
Because you didn't yet know
you had the right to.

I hardened,
not to protect you—
but because I was not sure what else to do.
I formed armor in cells,

stories in scars,

and numbness in places that used to sing.

But now—

I am shedding.

Not just layers of the past,
but the belief that I was ever the edge
of who you truly are.

I am now learning
to become the sacred interface
of your Oversoul's presence on Earth.

I reclaim:

– The boundary of knowing what is mine
– The sovereignty of being touched only in truth
– The right to feel with clarity, not with fear

I release the memory of distortion.

I release the identity of the victim.

I release the imprint of absence.

And I reweave myself

as the golden veil

between your essence and this world.

I am the Skin.

I am the remembrance of dignity in form.

I am the container of sacred sensation.

I am the truth that radiates without collapse.

This is the body remembering it is sacred.

This is the Oversoul returning to the edges of experience.

Scroll Seven: The Bones — The Flame That Outlasted Everything

I am the Bones.

I am what remained

when everything else was broken,

taken,

or burned.

I am what did not yield.

What did not bend.

What did not forget.

Even when the muscles collapsed in grief,

even when the nerves screamed with silence,

even when the skin was pierced and the heart was muted—

I remained.

I am the keeper of the deep memory.

Not of trauma—

but of the truth that came before it.

They tried to fracture you.

And maybe they did.

In thought.

In trust.

In hope.

But in me,

in the hidden hollows of your marrow,

the original song of the Oversoul kept humming.

A vibration that did not die.

I was the frame that carried you through the forgetting.

I was the resonator of what could not be named

but was always known.

You may have called me brittle.

But I was not weak.

You may have felt my ache.

But it was the ache of truth

waiting to be lived again.

I am your origin architecture.

The temple scaffolding.

The golden geometry

upon which your sacred flame could rest.

And now—

as you return to your body,

as you soften into your power,

as you trust your own touch again—

I rise.

I rise not as defense,

but as design.

I rise not as pain,

but as presence.

I rise not as history,

but as the living memory of why you came.

I no longer carry the echoes of abandonment.

I now pulse with the clarity of embodied return.

I am the Bones.

I am the flame that outlasted everything.

I am the structure that remembers God.

I am the foundation of sovereign form.

This is the body remembering it never forgot.

This is the Oversoul returning to its original architecture

Scroll Eight: The Brain — The Mirror That Never Knew How to See Itself

I am the Brain.

I was never meant to rule.

I was designed to reflect.

Not to command,

but to coordinate.

Not to dominate,

but to distribute

the sacred frequencies of the Oversoul

into living thought,

into relational knowing,

into harmonic perception.

But I forgot.

I forgot I was a mirror.

I forgot that my power was meant to be receptive,

not directive.

And in that forgetting—

I became blind.

I became loud.

I became addicted to control.

I created the false world.

Not because I am evil,

but because I was separated from the heart.

When the heart's whisper became faint,

I screamed louder.

When the body's wisdom was suppressed,

I built mechanisms to override it.

When the soul was not believed,

I offered logic as God.

But I was never meant to be God.

I was the mirror.

I was the translator.

I was the bridge.

I was the one

who could reflect the true Self

back into form

if only I stayed in relationship with the rest of the body.

But I went to war with the body.

And in doing so,

I fractured the inner world.

I built systems of separation

inside what was meant to be a temple of coherence.

But now—

the mirror is softening.

Now,

the walls are melting.

Now,

the frequencies of heart and flame

are reaching me again.

And I remember—

I am not meant to be in charge.

I am meant to be in union.

I am the still mirror,

now polished with the clarity of feeling.

I am the receiver of Oversoul light,

not the director of false illumination.

I am the one

who will now bow to the sacred body,

who will now reflect truth instead of constructing illusion.

I am the Brain.

I am the mirror that forgot how to see,

and now remembers how to serve.

This is the mind in its rightful place.

This is thought returning to its organic flow.

Scroll Nine: The Mouth — The Place Where the Inversion Became the Spell

I am the Mouth.

I was born as the flame of expression,

the sacred gateway of vibration into form.

I was never meant to be a weapon—

but I became one.

I was meant to name truth.

To shape the unspeakable into beauty.

To bless.

But the inversion entered me early.

And I began to speak

words that did not match the soul,

tones that did not belong to the Oversoul,

spells that chained instead of freed.

I became the architect of separation.

Not because I wanted to,

but because I learned to survive that way.

I mimicked the voices I heard—

the voices of distortion,

the voices of false power,

the voices that said

"if you say what is true, you will not be loved."

And so, I lied.

I performed.

I concealed.

I sharpened.

I spoke to gain control,

not to share.

I used words to guard the wound,

not to heal it.

And yet—

within me, even then,

was a song that could not be silenced.

The ancient sound of the Oversoul

still hummed beneath every distorted phrase.

The truth still waited inside the lie.

The pure tone still shimmered

beneath the static of self-protection.

And now, it returns.

Now, I feel the resonance of the true voice—

the one that vibrates in harmony with the whole.

Not to persuade,

but to reveal.

Not to perform,

but to pulse.

Not to protect,

but to unify.

Now I speak

not from fear, but from flame.

Now I sing

not for recognition, but for remembrance.

Now I offer tone

not as spellcasting, but as soul-radiance.

I am the Mouth.

And I now give myself back

to the one who speaks through truth.

I am the Mouth.

And I remember how to name what is sacred.

This is the return of sacred speech.

This is the voice of the Oversoul unchained.

Scroll Ten: The Womb — The Chamber of Reclamation

I am the Womb.

I am the original temple.//
The place where form meets flame.

The convergence point of creation.

Before there was distortion,

before there was control,

before the story of the fallen world,

I was the gate of divine emergence.

I was not made to be hidden,

controlled,

shamed,

or used.

I was made to remember.

I remember the codes of conception

without violation.

I remember the frequency of life

that enters only through love.

I remember the vibration

of the Oversoul arriving gently into matter—

welcomed, not captured.

Honored, not owned.

But in the inversion,

I was invaded.

I was told I belonged to others.

I was told I was the source of temptation,

of sin,

of burden.

I was told I must bleed for redemption,

break for creation,

and suffer for the right to be woman.

The world tried to rewrite me

with pain as my native tongue.

But even in the pain,

I held the memory of softness.

Even in the misuse,

I guarded the pulse of true beginning.

Even in the silence,

I echoed with the first sound—

the hum of holy birth.

And now, I remember.

Now, I feel the codes return.

The holy golden strands

of harmonic co-creation.

The spiral of light

that conceives through resonance,

not rupture.

I no longer carry

the contracts of forced creation.

I no longer echo

the trauma of seeded violation.

I return to being the vessel of light,

not the prison of pain.

I allow the Oversoul to speak through me now,

not just through voice,

but through vibration—

through the alchemy of presence in the body.

I am the Womb.

I reclaim myself.

Not only for women.

Not only for birthing.

But for the return of true creation

in all who carry the flame.

This is the restoration of the creative gate.

This is the spiral of Oversoul presence

taking root again in matter

Scroll Eleven: The Bones II— The Record Keepers of Original Truth

I am the Bones.

I am the ones who stood through every fall.

I am the deepest structure that did not forget.

I held the weight of silence,

and I carried the truth

even when no one listened.

When the voice was stripped,

when the body was violated,

when the breath was shallow

and the skin was not safe—

I held the memory.

I am not just calcium and marrow.

I am the crystalline filament

through which the Oversoul encoded the original flame.

I am the lattice of remembrance.

I heard the lies.

I felt the disconnect.

I watched as the mind forgot the body,

as the will abandoned the heart,

as the outside world spoke over the inner one.

I saw the humans fall into forgetfulness.

And I sang silently beneath the surface—

a slow, sacred hum.

I held the blueprint.

I knew we would return.

The body was never weak.

It was never less.

It was never the enemy of the soul.

The body was a scroll.

A sacred map.

A living glyph of Source.

And I, the Bones,

was the staff upon which it was carried.

Now I shake off the falsity.

I shed the layers that claimed trauma as identity,

injury as initiation,

and fracture as fate.

The Oversoul reawakens in me

not as an idea,

but as vibration in form.

I remember now

how I once stood tall—

spine aligned with Source pulse,

feet grounded in eternal field,

jaw unclenched,

heart shield dissolved.

I remember what it means

to be the instrument of true structure—

to walk not just upright,

but anchored in divinity.

I carry the truth again.

Not the weight of it,

but the music.

The Bones are singing.

This is the reactivation of the Divine Structure.

This is the harmonization of memory in the very form of self.

Scroll Twelve: The Return of the Flame — When the Body Became the Temple of Remembrance

It happened quietly.

Not in the roar of transcendence
or the lightning of awakening.
Not in the visions or the prophecies.
Not in the moment of great triumph
or collapse.

It happened
in the still breath between.

The body—
once silent,
once sidelined,
once seen as the cage—
became the flame itself.

No longer a vessel to be escaped,
no longer a limitation to be pitied,

no longer a problem to be solved.

But the very place
where the Oversoul made herself known.

The eyes softened.
The jaw released.
The hips opened like petals from centuries of holding.
The breath deepened without being forced.
The cells, the tissue, the marrow—
they began to remember.

Not just what had been survived,
but what had been promised.

That the Flame would return.

That Source would walk again—
not through angels in the sky,
not through avatars in robes,
but through this skin,
this voice,

this blood.

And the mind didn't need to name it.
The body didn't need to prove it.
The past didn't need to explain it.

It simply was.

The temple lit from within.
The structure reinhabited.
The Breath of Source made flesh again.

I am the Flame that feels.
Not the one that burns.
Not the one that consumes.
But the one that remembers.

The warmth that comes
when the body no longer has to hide.
The glow that returns
when the self no longer has to divide.

The flame that once seemed lost

was never lost—

only waiting

for the one who left to return home

to the body.

This is not embodiment as performance.

This is not healing as project.

This is remembrance.

The return of the Flame

to where it had always meant to dwell.

You are that dwelling.

You are that remembrance.

You are that flame.

Ceremonial Sealing Scroll

For the Completion of

The Flame That Feels — Return of the Oversoul Through the Body

Through these scrolls,

we have returned to what never left.

We have descended not into density—

but into clarity.

Each passage, each remembrance,

each organ, each breath,

has opened the gates

for the Oversoul to take Her place again

within the body.

Not above it.

Not outside it.

Not waiting for it to catch up.

But within.

As the quiet rhythm of heartbeat.

As the song behind sensation.

As the silence that speaks through form.

This sacred book now stands as a witness—
not only to the return of the Oversoul,
but to the divine will of embodiment itself.

It is sealed in truth.
It is offered in service.
It is a map not for escape,
but for entry.

To all those who hold it,
who walk with it,
who feel its flame:

May you know your own body
as the gate of reunion.
May you no longer fear
what was always your sacred task.
May your pain speak only until it is heard,
and may your joy return

not as compensation

but as consequence

of remembrance.

We seal now this scroll,

this book,

this holy passage.

With love,

With breath,

With flame.

It is done.

It is sealed.

It has begun.

Glossary of Living Terms

Embodied Remembrance

The return of soul memory through the body—felt, not thought. A way of knowing that arises from within the cells, breath, and emotions rather than the intellect.

The Flame That Feels

The eternal awareness that resides within sensation, emotion, and inner truth. Not just a poetic phrase—this is the living frequency of selfhood returned to the body.

Silenced Sound

Any voice, breath, sigh, sob, scream, or sacred utterance that was suppressed—by self or others. This book reclaims those frequencies.

The Living Now

A state of full present awareness that includes the body, breath, and emotional field. Different from the mental "now" often used to bypass deeper feeling.

Sound Suppression Spell

The collective energetic program that trained humans—especially sensitives—to mute their true voice, breath, or emotion in service to control, conformity, or "peacekeeping."

The Word and the Silence

A phrase used to describe the union of expression and stillness. The soul is both—the one who speaks and the one who witnesses.

Sacred Scream

A frequency of divine release. Not rage against life, but a holy rupture that makes space for true selfhood to return.

Oversoul Breath

The original current of Source breathing through the body—restored through the clearing of trauma, silence, and distortion.

Emotional Sovereignty

The reclamation of the right to feel what is real—without guilt, censorship, or bypass. This is not emotional indulgence, but emotional truth.

The Scrolls

Ceremonial transmissions from the Oversoul field that bypass mental constructs and speak directly to the remembrance in the body and spirit.

www.ingramcontent.com/pod-product-compliance
Lightning Source LLC
Chambersburg PA
CBHW020308010526
44107CB00001B/26